RECORDED VERSIONS GUITAR

AUTHENTIC TRANSCRIPTIONS WITH NOTES AND TABLATURE

THE BEST OF Duane Eddy

Transcribed by Dave Whitehill

HAL•LEONARD® CORPORATION

7777 W. BLUEMOUND RD. P.O. BOX 13819 MILWAUKEE, WI 53213

Visit Hal Leonard Online at
www.halleonard.com

Photo by Tom Bert

Duane Eddy, the most successful and influential instrumentalist in Rock and Roll history, is the man who added a new term to the American music dictionary — *Twang*. The sound he created, using his trademark red Gretsch guitar, was easily identifiable and uniquely his own. Combining strong, dramatic, single-note melodies, along with bending of the low strings, he produced a sound that was unlike anything yet heard — the sound that would be featured on an unprecedented string of thirty-four chart singles and sales of over 100 million worldwide.

In the early days of Rock and Roll, the notion of the lead guitarist as the charismatic figure in the spotlight was completely novel, but Duane Eddy moved the guitar player front and center. Quiet and unassuming offstage, he cut an indelible figure with an electric guitar in his hands. It was a classic pose that defined the cool iconography of what it means to be a *Rock and Roller*.

Born in Corning, New York, in 1938, he began playing at age five, emulating his cowboy hero, Gene Autry. The family moved West to Phoenix, Arizona, in the early Fifties, where Duane met his longtime partner, co-writer and producer, Lee Hazlewood. Together, they created a successful formula based upon Duane's unique approach to his instrument, and Lee's experimental vision in the recording studio, and have been referred to as "one of the greatest hit-making machines of the Rock and Roll era."

9 years old – upstate New York

Elements of country, blues, jazz, and gospel infused his instrumentals. They had evocative titles like, "Rebel 'Rouser," "Forty Miles of Bad Road," "Cannonball," "The Lonely One," "Shazam," and "Some Kinda' Earthquake." They were filled with rebel yells and brilliant sax breaks. The worldwide popularity of these records, beginning with "Moovin' and Groovin'" in 1958, broke open the doors

for Rock and Roll instrumental music. His band, The Rebels, featured musicians who were to become some of the world's best-known session players. Sax players Steve Douglas and Jim Horn, and pianist Larry Knechtel, have been heard on hundreds of hit records, becoming members of the famous "Wrecking Crew" of Phil Spector in the Sixties, and touring with a very elite group of artists through the years.

"Peter Gunn" session with Steve Douglas on Sax – Phoenix, AZ, 1959.

The following decade was a blur of touring and recording, with an astonishing amount of work being released. Duane constantly broke new ground, producing over 25 albums spanning a broad range of themes. At the height of the Rock and Roll era, he recorded an album of completely acoustic music, *Songs of Our Heritage*, the first "unplugged" project, so to speak. There were orchestral projects, Big Band sounds of the Forties, and an album of songs written by a young man, who, years later, would thank Duane for "doin' my songs" — apparently, Bob Dylan liked what he heard.

The Seventies were equally as busy for Duane. He produced album projects for Phil Everly and Waylon Jennings. A collaboration with hit songwriter Tony Macaulay led to a worldwide top ten record, "Play Me Like You Play Your Guitar". The single record, "You Are My Sunshine," featuring Willie Nelson and Waylon Jennings, hit the country charts in 1977.

An amazing group of legendary players hit the road in early 1983, showing up at small, intimate clubs. Friends of Duane's, some old, some new, had put this

band together wanting to give the fans a chance to hear him in a unique setting — Don Randi on keyboards, Hal Blaine on drums, Steve Douglas on sax, and to Duane's pleasant surprise, Ry Cooder on guitar. Needless to say, this group *rocked*, and the lines around

Duane Eddy (3rd from left),
16 years old with his first electric guitar –
Arizona, 1954

the blocks and the superb reviews said it all. Duane Eddy was back, and a whole new generation of fans were listening.

In 1986, Duane recorded with Art of Noise, a collaboration that brought a new twist to his 1960 best seller, "Peter Gunn." The song was an instant, Top Ten hit around the world, ranking #1 on *Rolling Stone Magazine's* dance chart for six weeks that summer. As further confirmation of it's success, "Peter Gunn" won the Grammy for Best Rock Instrumental of 1986.

The following year, a new album, the self-titled, *Duane Eddy*, was released on Capitol. As a tribute to his influence and inspiration to so many young players, a crowd of unbelievable talent came along to be a part of this project. Tracks were produced by Paul McCartney, Jeff Lynne, Ry Cooder, Art of Noise, and Duane. The "band" included John Fogerty, George Harrison, Paul McCartney, Ry Cooder, James Burton, David Lindley, Steve Cropper, and original Rebels, Larry Knechtel and Jim Horn. In the Spring of 1994, Duane Eddy's place in our musical history was etched in stone at his induction into The Rock and Roll Hall of Fame, alongside fellow artists Elton John, Rod Stewart, John Lennon, Bob Marley, and The Grateful Dead. Later that year, film soundtracks brought Duane's guitar to millions as they watched *Forrest Gump* being chased by a pickup truck

Brooklyn Fox Theater, Alan Freed show, 1958

full of rednecks, running into his football career to the sound of "Rebel 'Rouser." Oliver Stone's *Natural Born Killers* used "The Trembler," a track written by Duane and Ravi Shankar, to help create a spine-chilling scene set against a violent thunderstorm in the desert.

In more recent film work, Duane joined Academy Award winning composer, Hans Zimmer, on the soundtrack of *Broken Arrow*, starring John Travolta. Duane was his first choice to be the voice for the villain's theme. To quote Mr. Zimmer, "I always thought that Duane's style was being ripped off by the spaghetti westerns. This time I got the real thing." The appeal of this theme, a dark and moody piece, has caused it to be used, once again, in an altogether different kind of film — the incredibly successful *Scream 2*.

In recognition of his contributions to the art and style of guitar players around the world, Gretsch has recently introduced *The Duane Eddy Signature Model 6120*. Detailed to his specifications, it is an exact reissue of the very first guitar that originally gave us the unique sound of Duane Eddy.

"The Twang Is Still the Thang"

England, 1987 –
photo by George Harrison

Ballad of Paladin
(Closing Theme from HAVE GUN WILL TRAVEL)

Music by Bernard Hermann

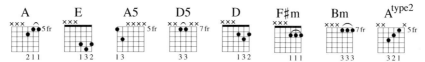

Gtr. 1; Drop D Tuning:
①= E ④= D
②= B ⑤= A
③= G ⑥= D

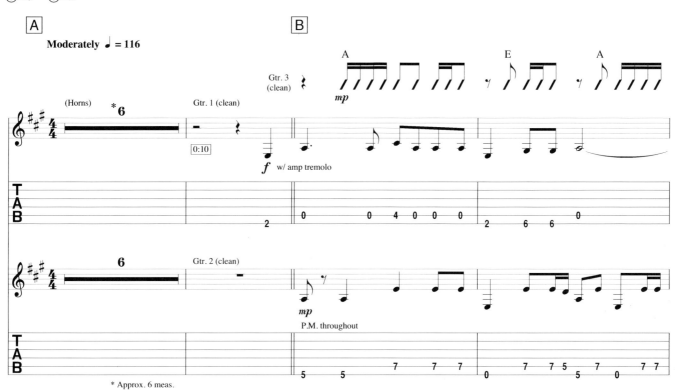

* Approx. 6 meas.

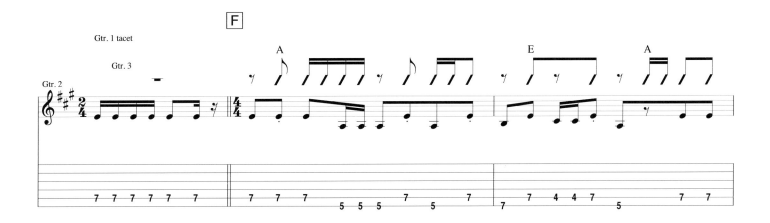

Because They're Young

Lyric by Aaron Schroeder and Wally Gold
Music by Don Costa

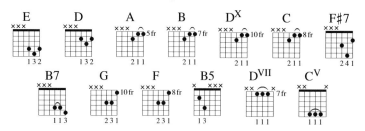

*Baritone gtr. tuned an octave lower than standard tuning.

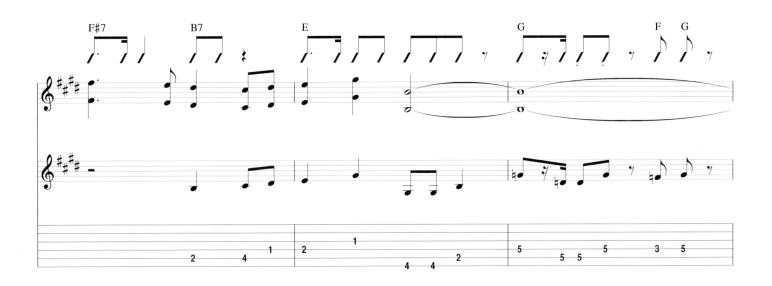

15

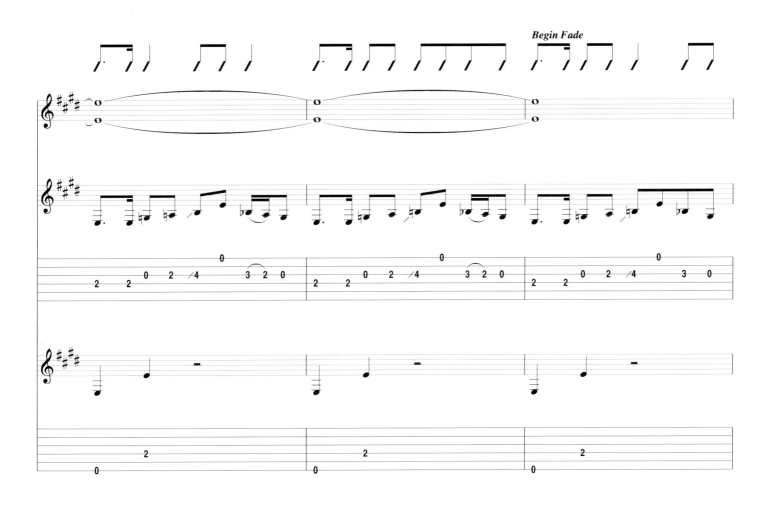

Bonnie Come Back

By Duane Eddy and Lee Hazlewood

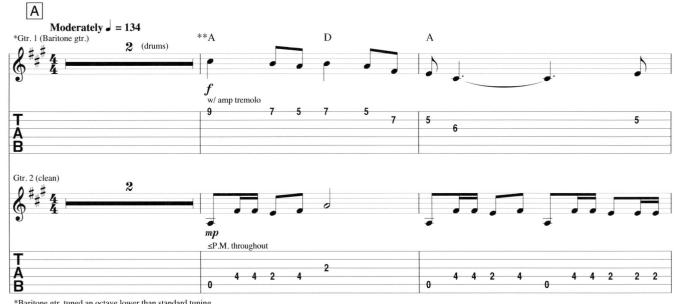

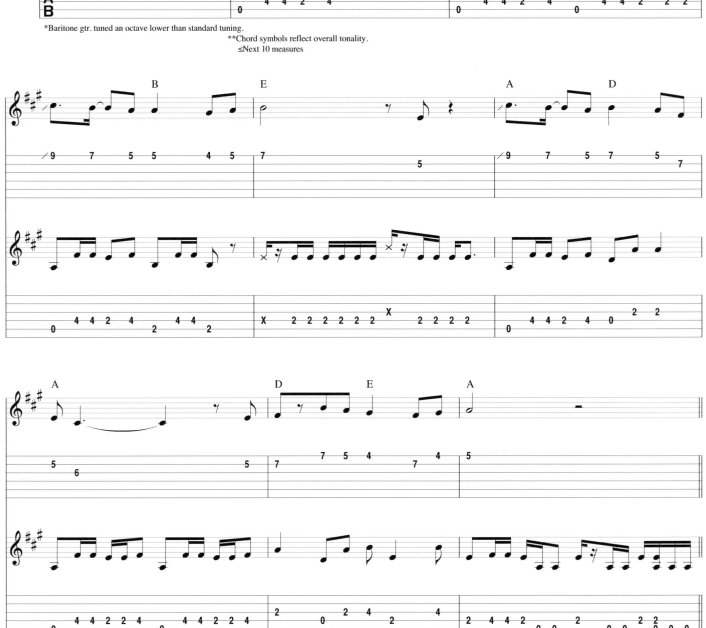

*Baritone gtr. tuned an octave lower than standard tuning.

**Chord symbols reflect overall tonality.

≤Next 10 measures

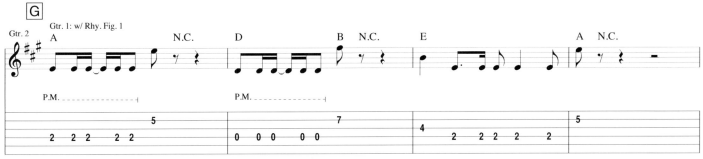

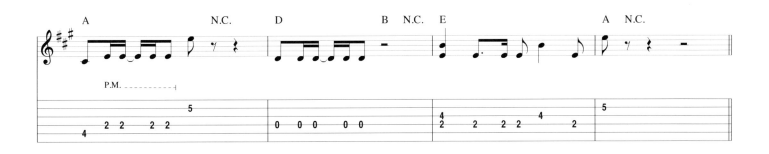

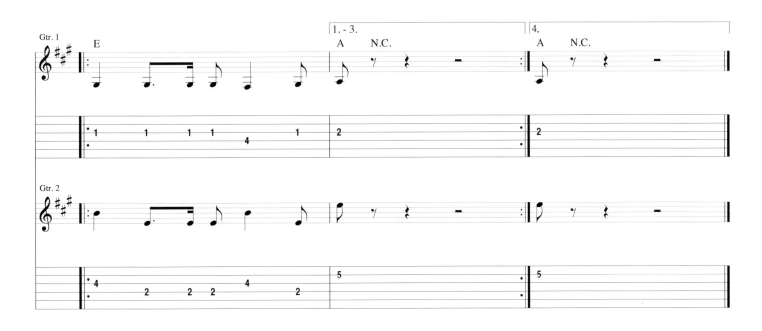

Boss Guitar

By Duane Eddy and Lee Hazlewood

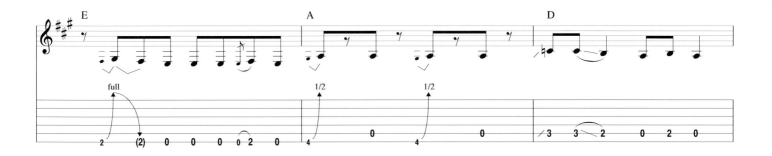

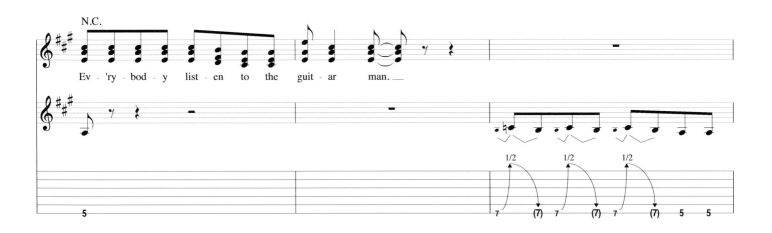

Ev - 'ry - bod - y list - en to the guit - ar man. _

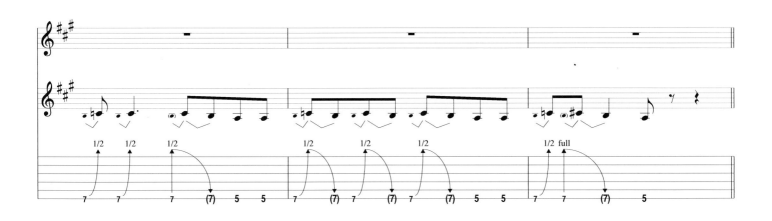

Bridge

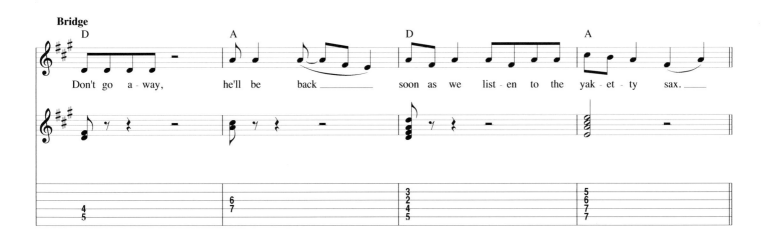

Don't go a - way, he'll be back _____ soon as we list - en to the yak - et - ty sax. _

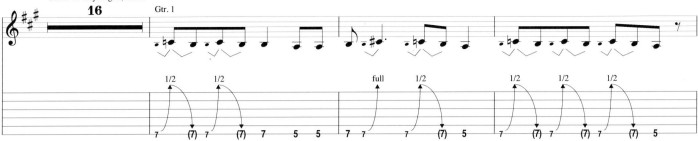

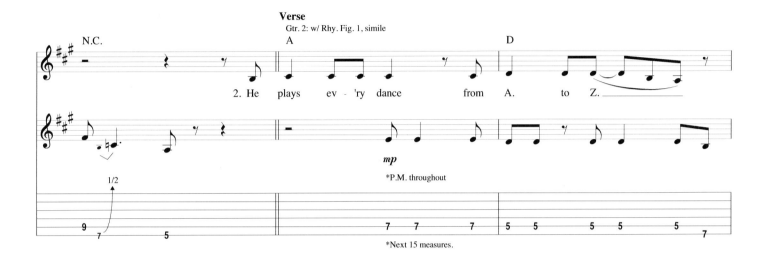

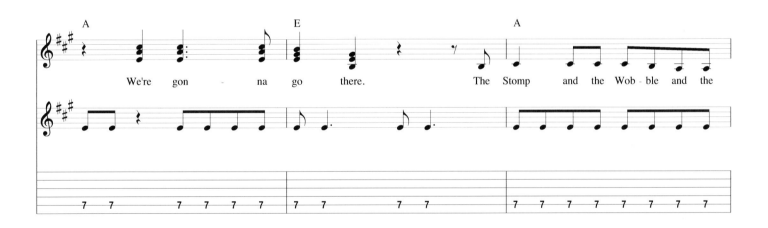

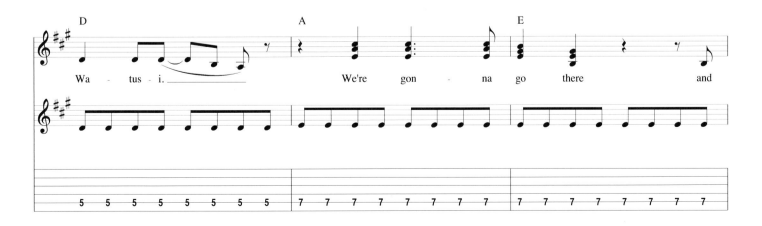

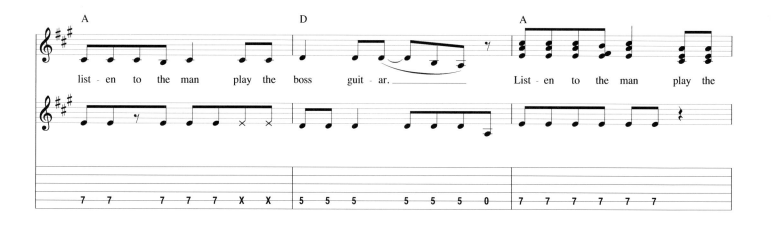

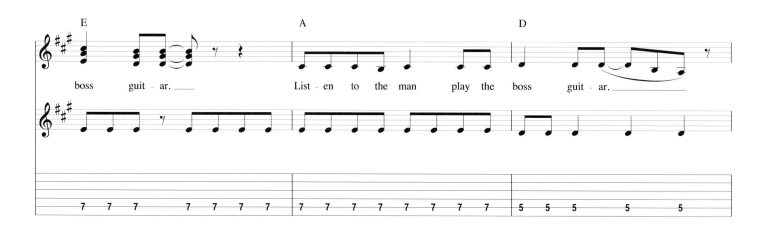

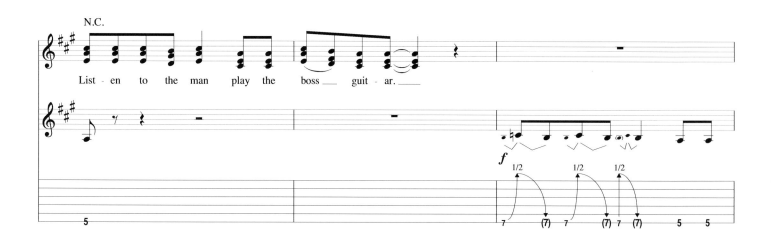

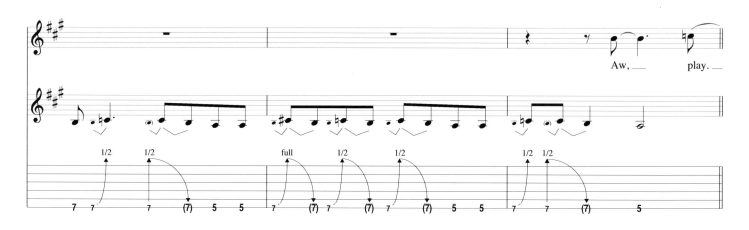

Outro

Buckaroo

By Bob Morris

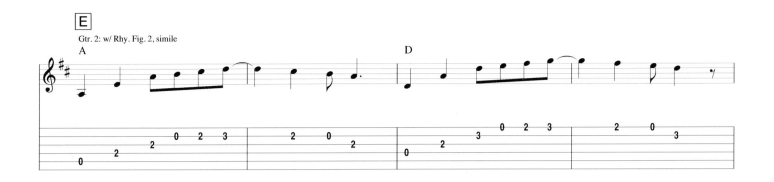

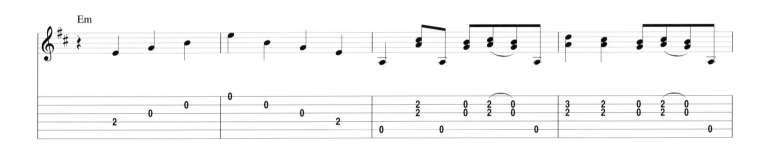

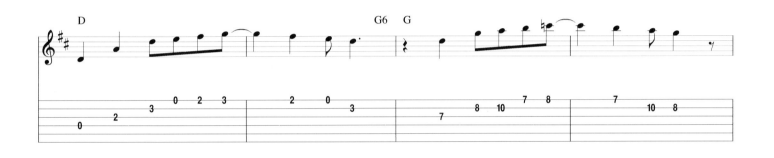

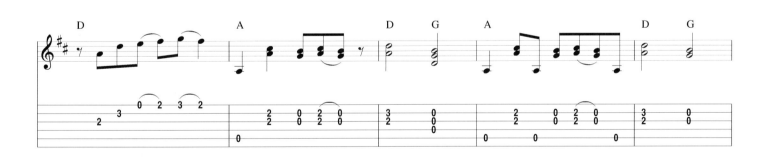

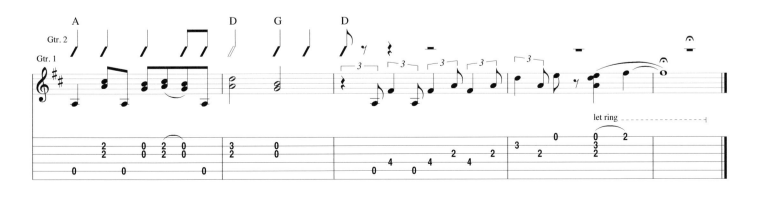

Cannonball

By Duane Eddy and Lee Hazlewood

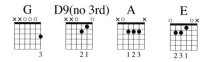

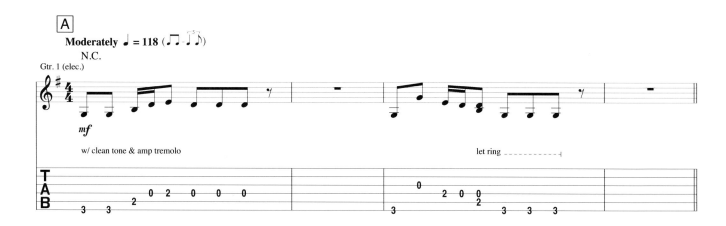

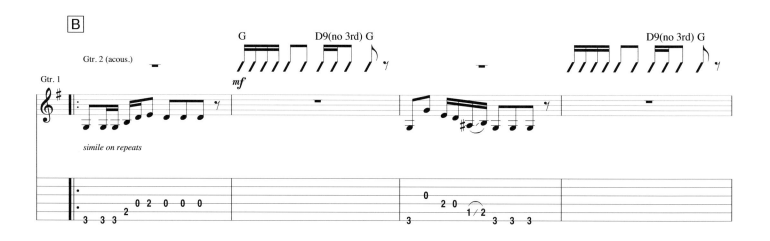

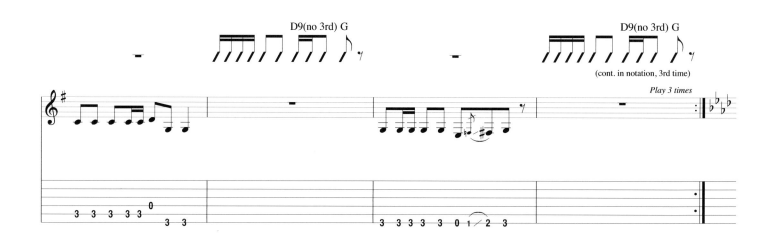

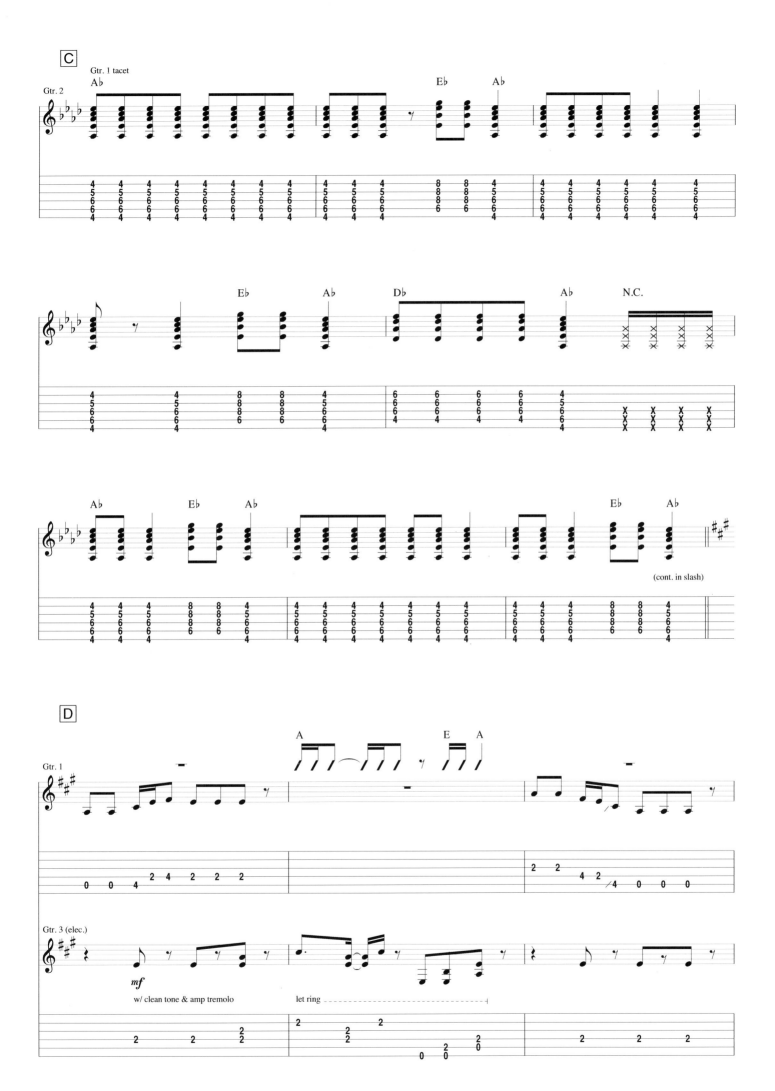

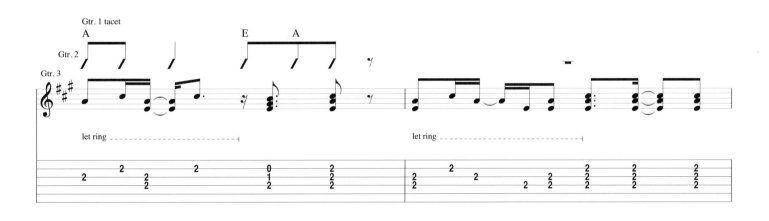

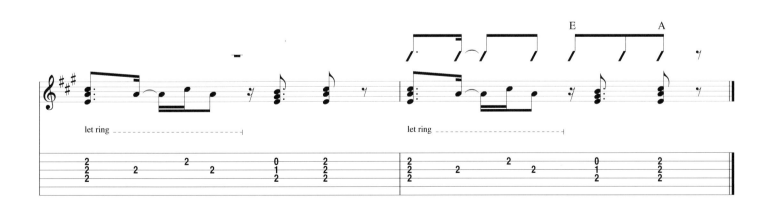

(Dance with The) Guitar Man

By Duane Eddy and Lee Hazlewood

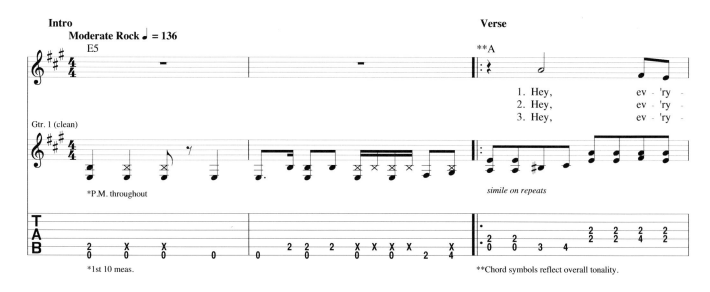

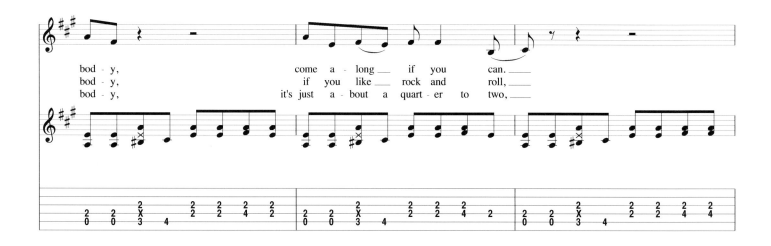

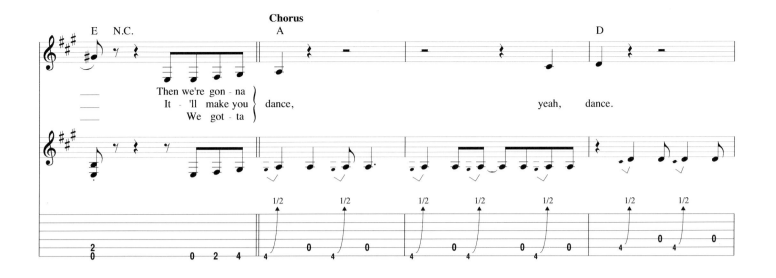

Chorus

Then we're gon - na
It - 'll make you dance,
We got - ta

yeah, dance.

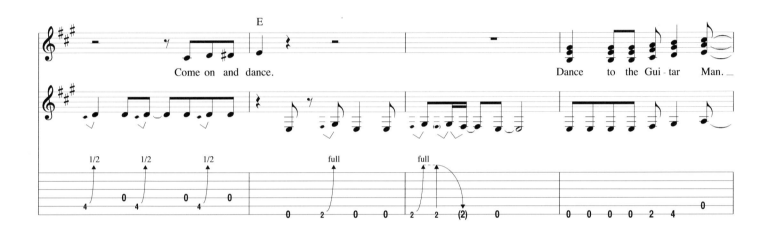

Come on and dance.

Dance to the Gui - tar Man.

Guitar Solo

Gtr. 1: w/ Fill 1, 2nd time

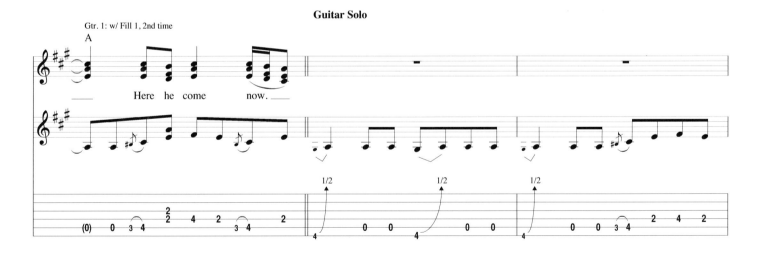

Here he come now.

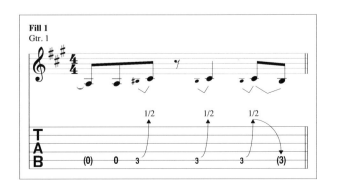

Fill 1
Gtr. 1

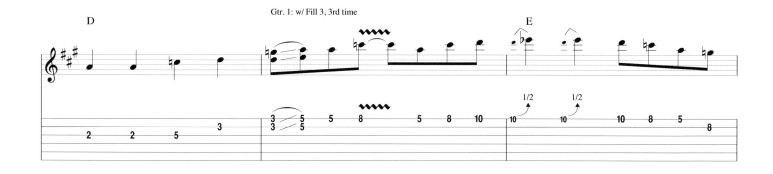

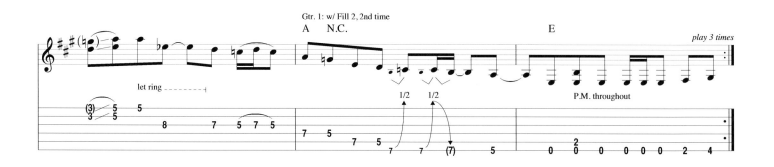

Outro

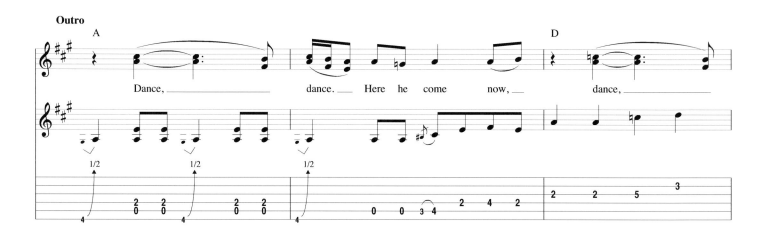

Dance, _____ dance. ___ Here he come now, _____ dance, _____

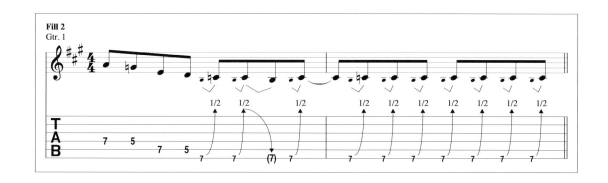

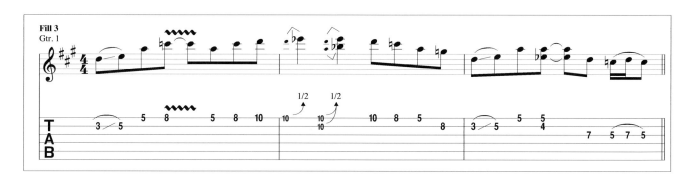

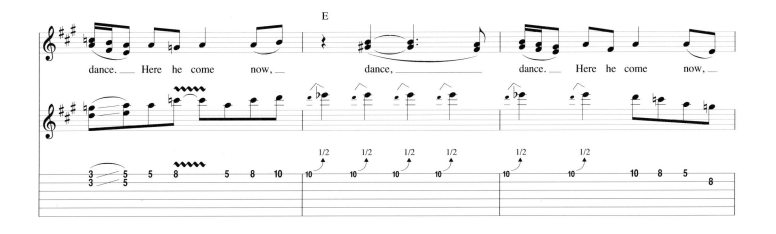

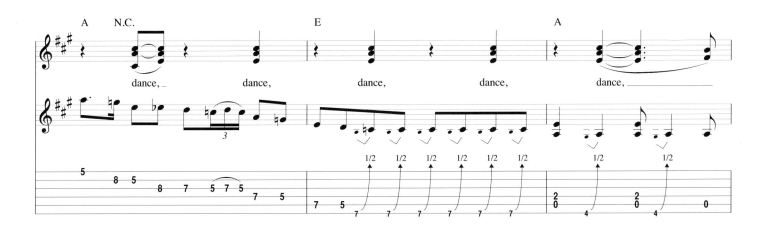

Forty Miles of Bad Road

By Duane Eddy and Al Casey

*Baritone gtr. tuned an octave lower than standard tuning. Written an octave higher throughout.

**Chord symbols reflect overall tonality.

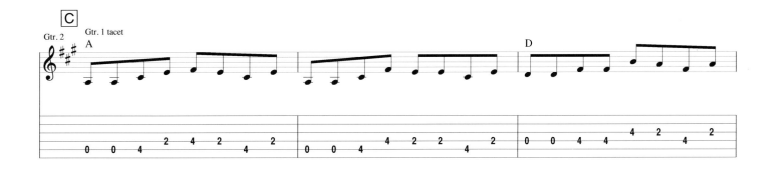

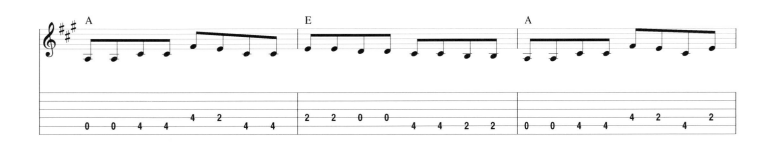

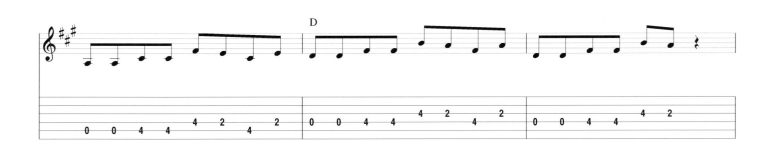

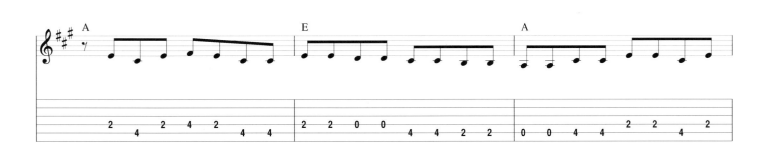

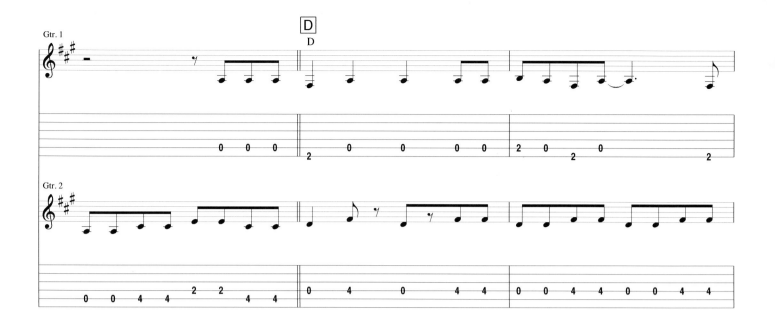

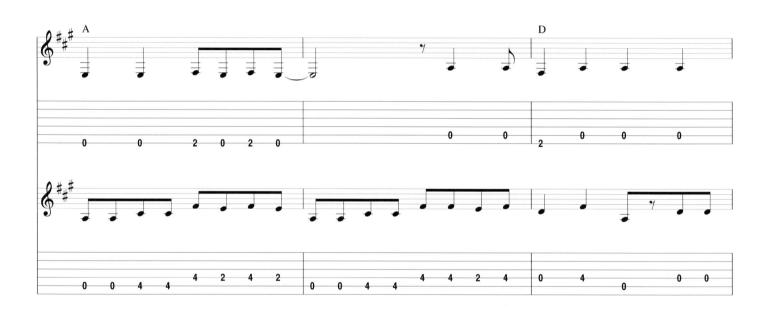

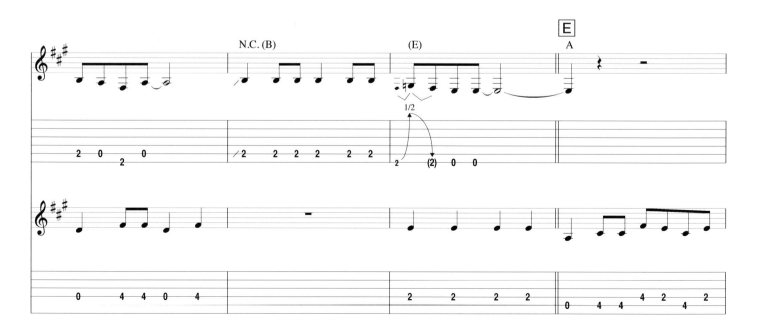

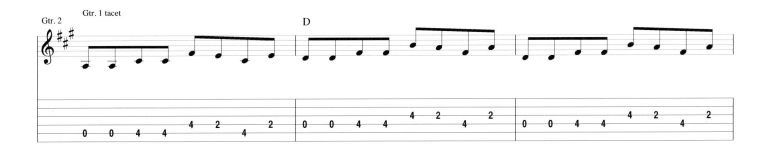

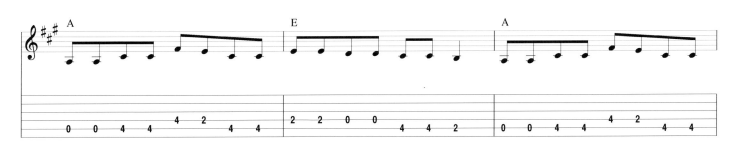

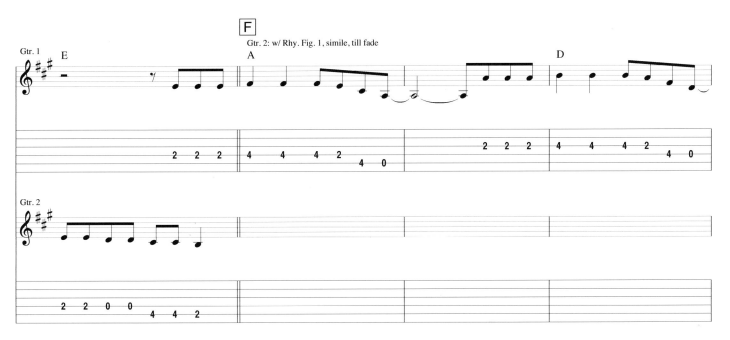

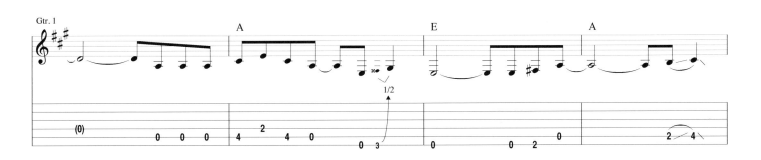

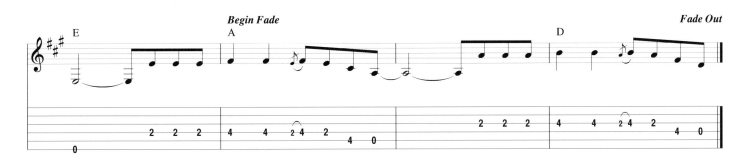

Kommotion

By Duane Eddy and Lee Hazlewood

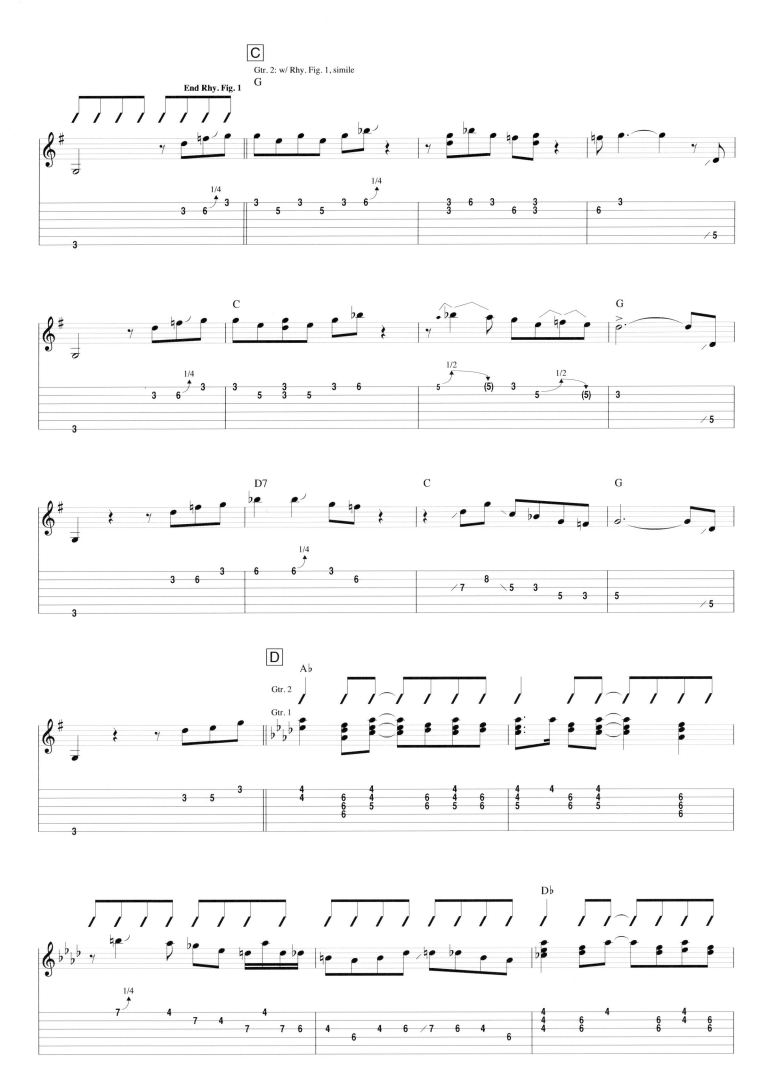

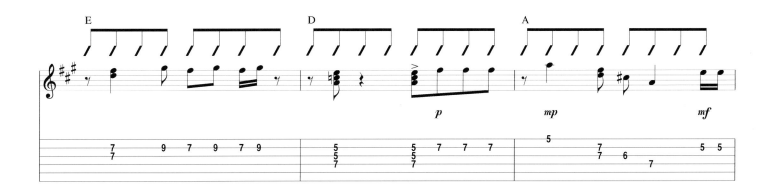

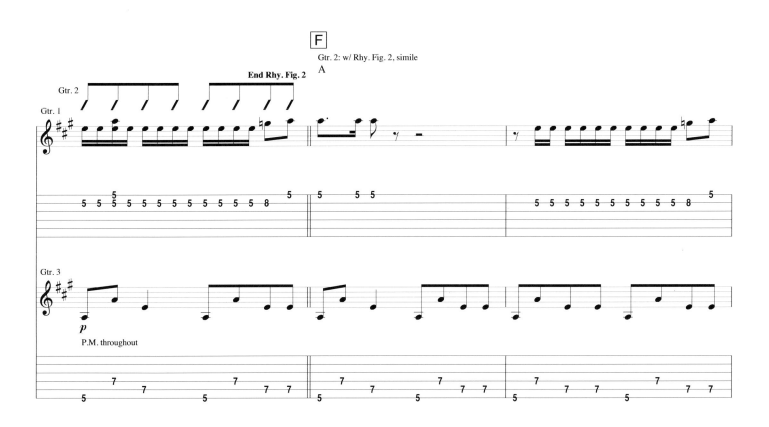

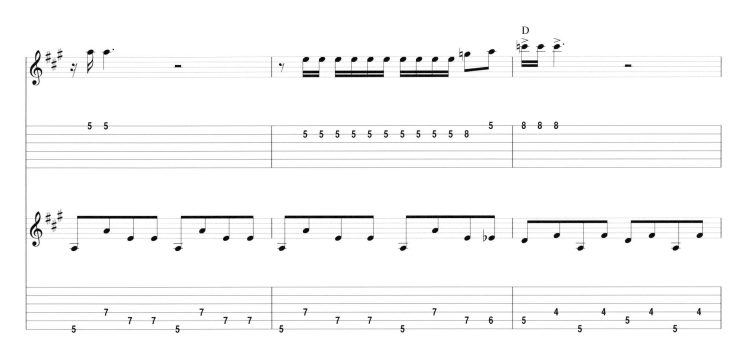

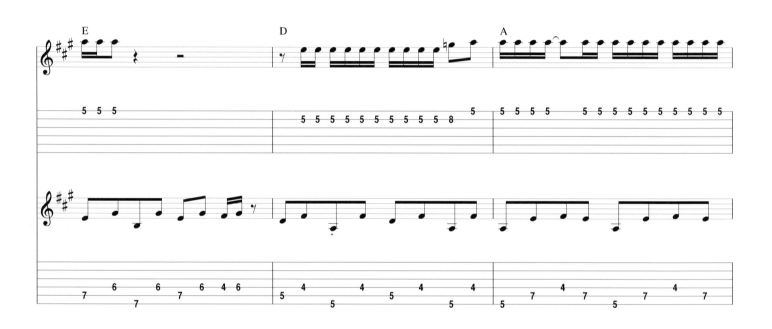

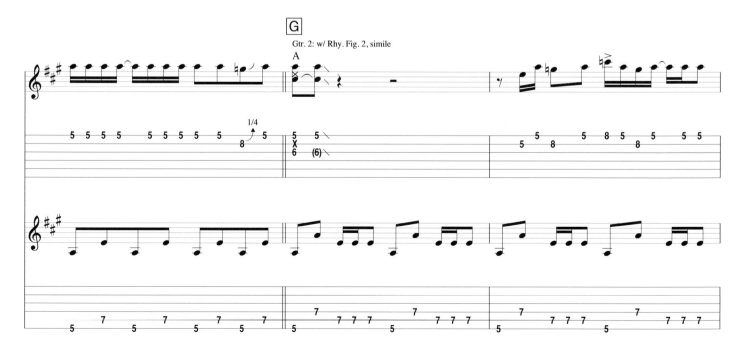

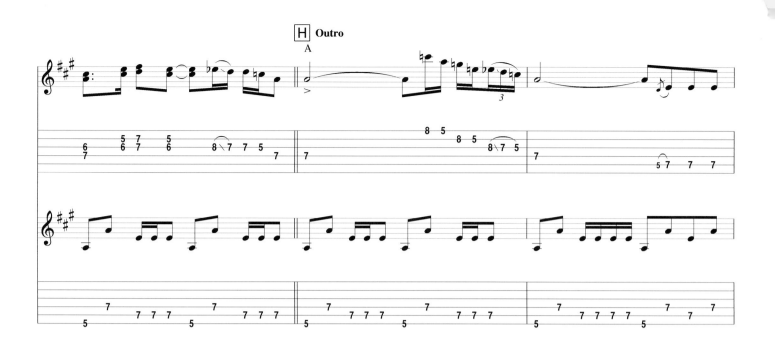

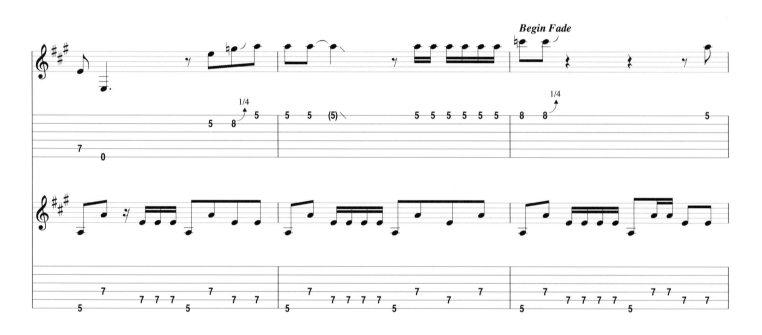

Pepe (Andalusian Girl)

Words by Dory Langdon
Music by Hans Wittstatt

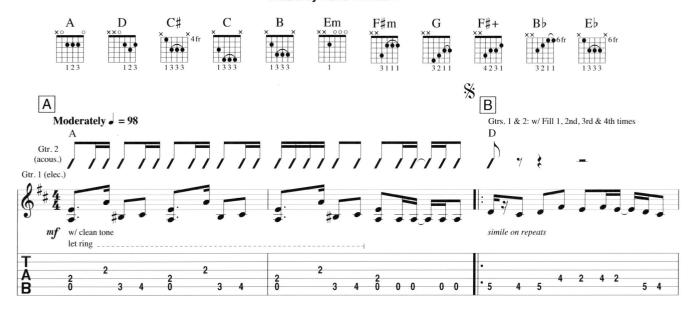

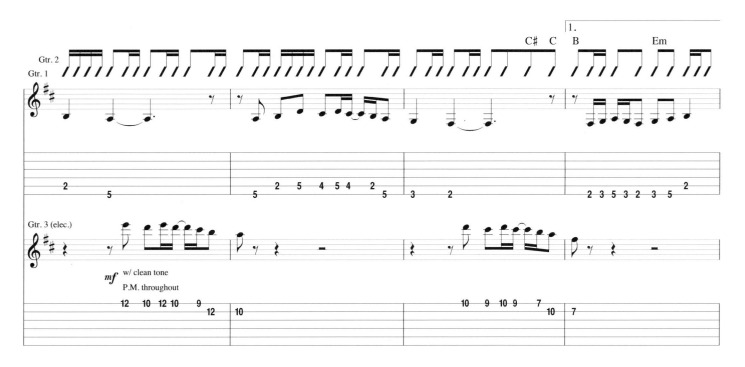

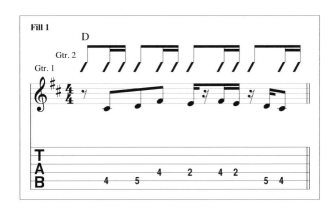

51

The Lonely One

By Duane Eddy and Lee Hazlewood

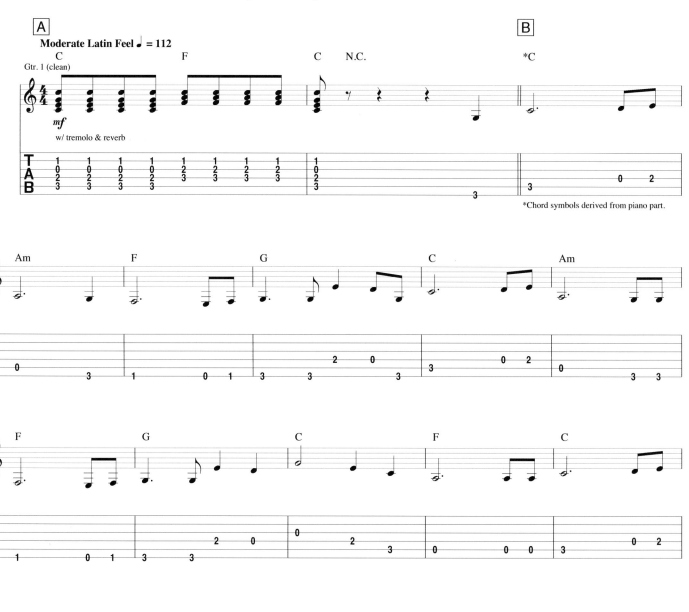

*Chord symbols derived from piano part.

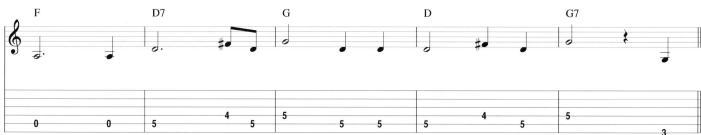

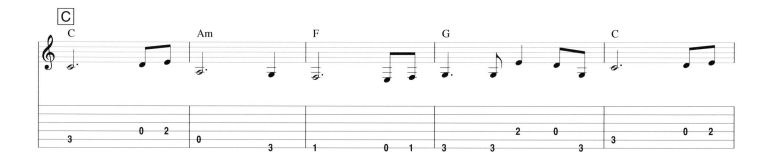

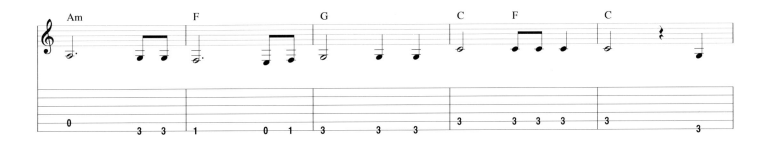

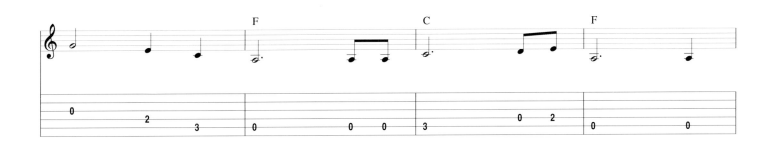

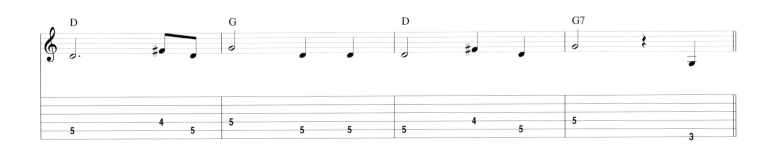

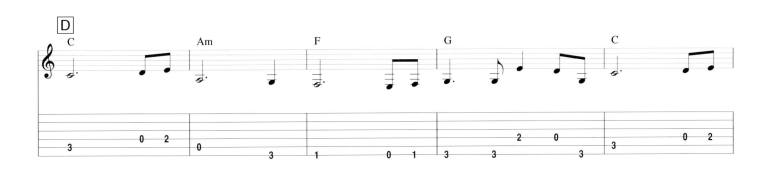

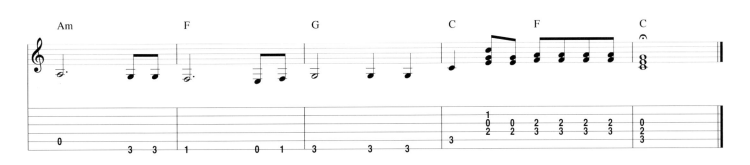

Peter Gunn

By Henry Mancini

Tune Up 1/2 Step:

①= F   ④= Eb

②= C   ⑤= Bb

③= Ab   ⑥= F

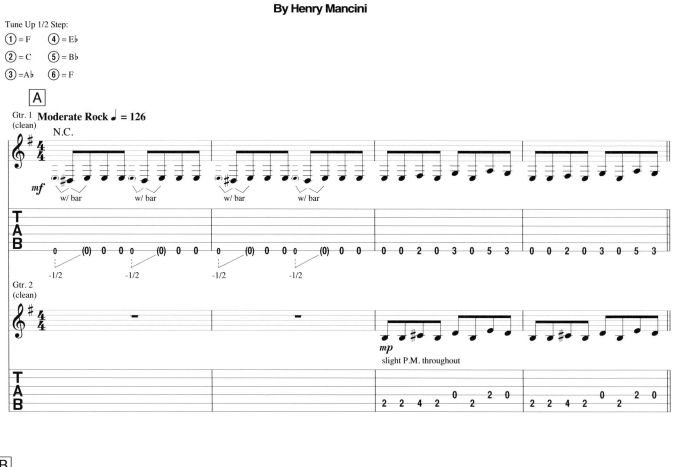

Ramrod

By Al Casey

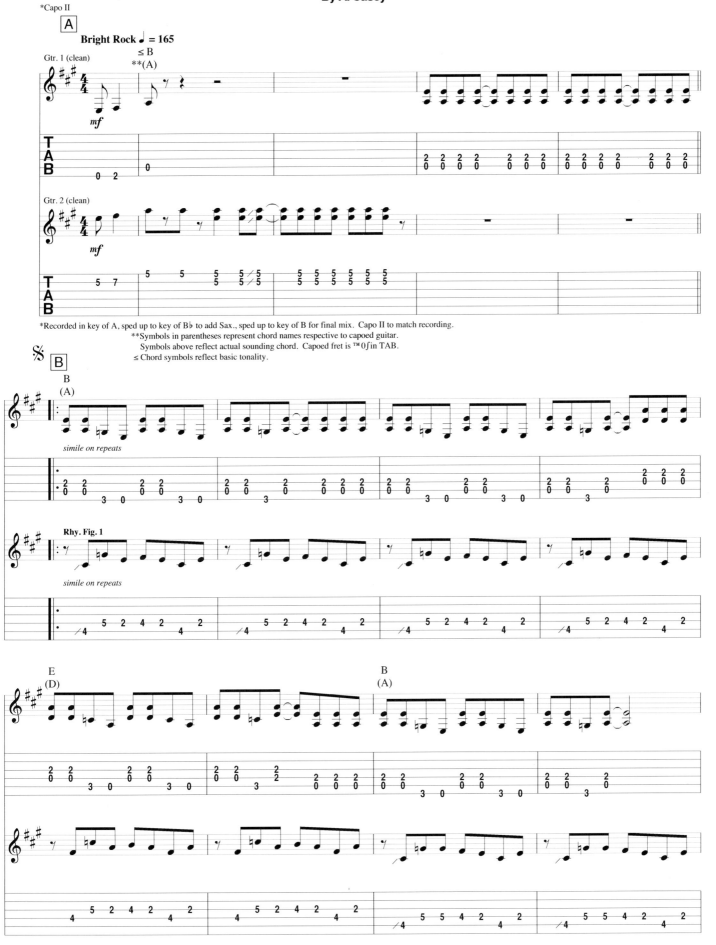

*Recorded in key of A, sped up to key of B♭ to add Sax., sped up to key of B for final mix. Capo II to match recording.

**Symbols in parentheses represent chord names respective to capoed guitar.
Symbols above reflect actual sounding chord. Capoed fret is ™0ƒin TAB.
≤ Chord symbols reflect basic tonality.

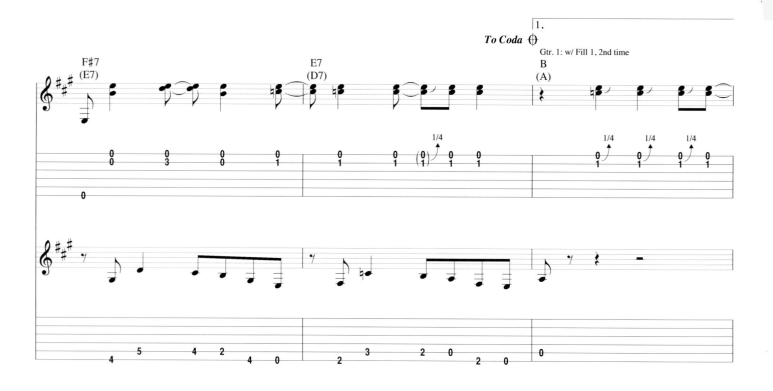

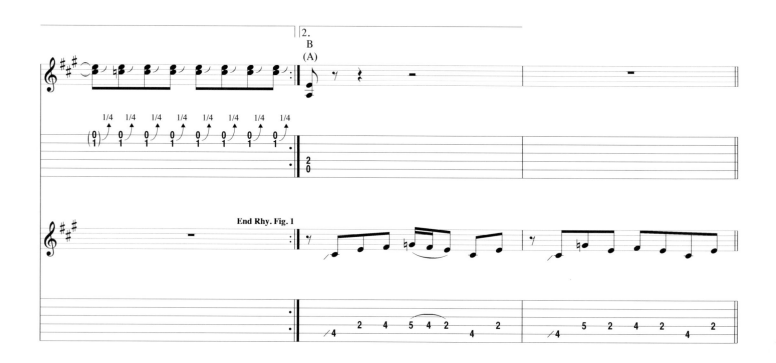

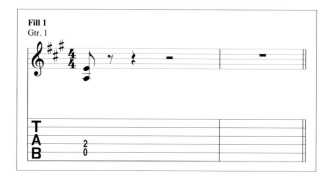

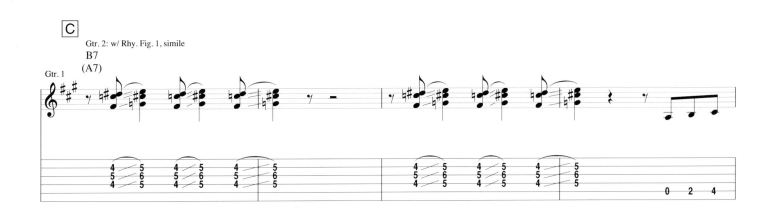

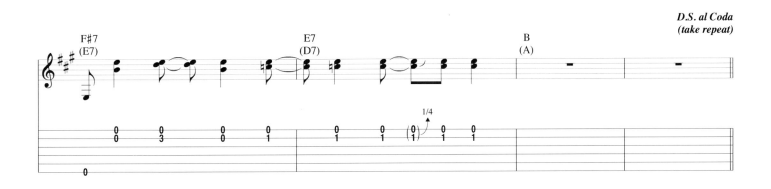

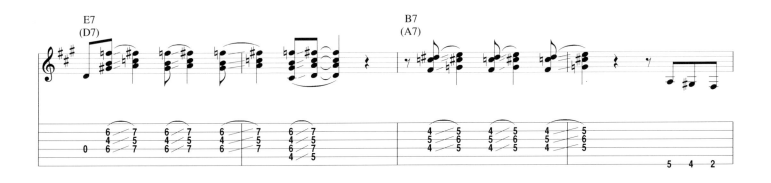

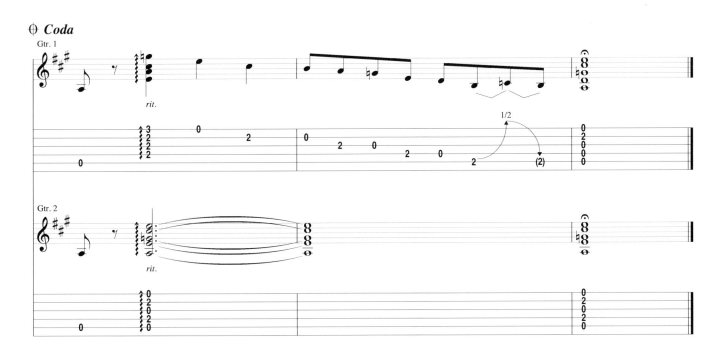

Rebel 'Rouser

By Duane Eddy and Lee Hazlewood

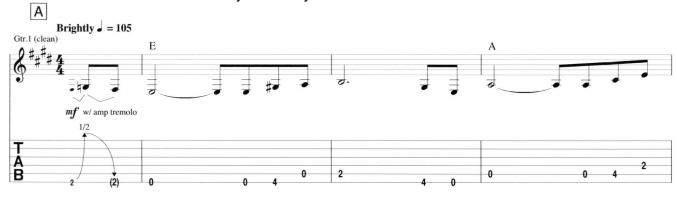

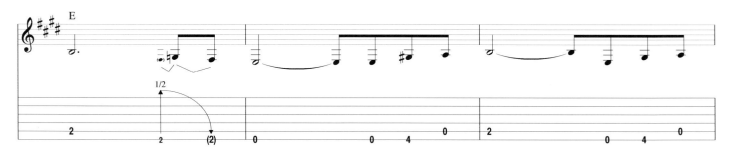

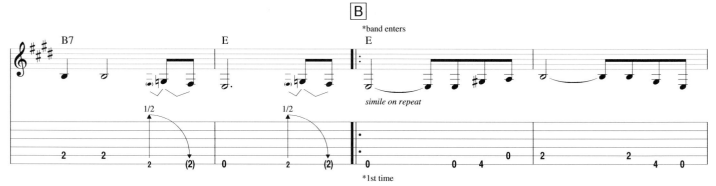

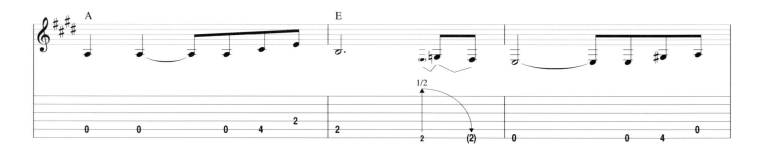

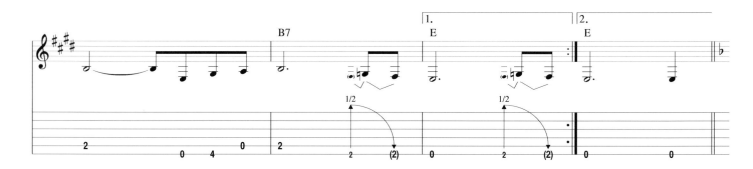

Shazam

By Duane Eddy and Lee Hazlewood

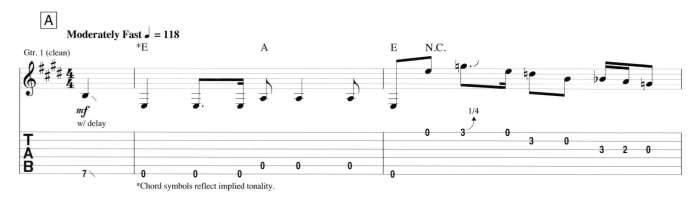

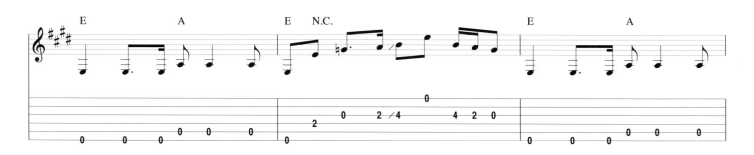

*Chord symbols reflect implied tonality.

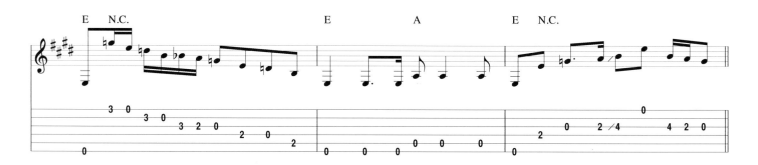

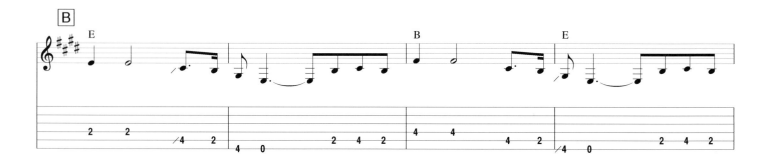

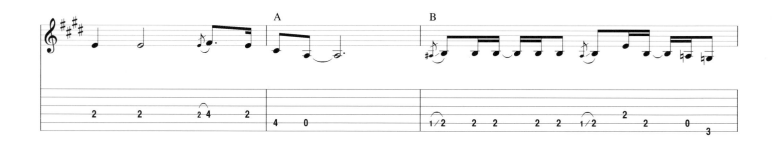

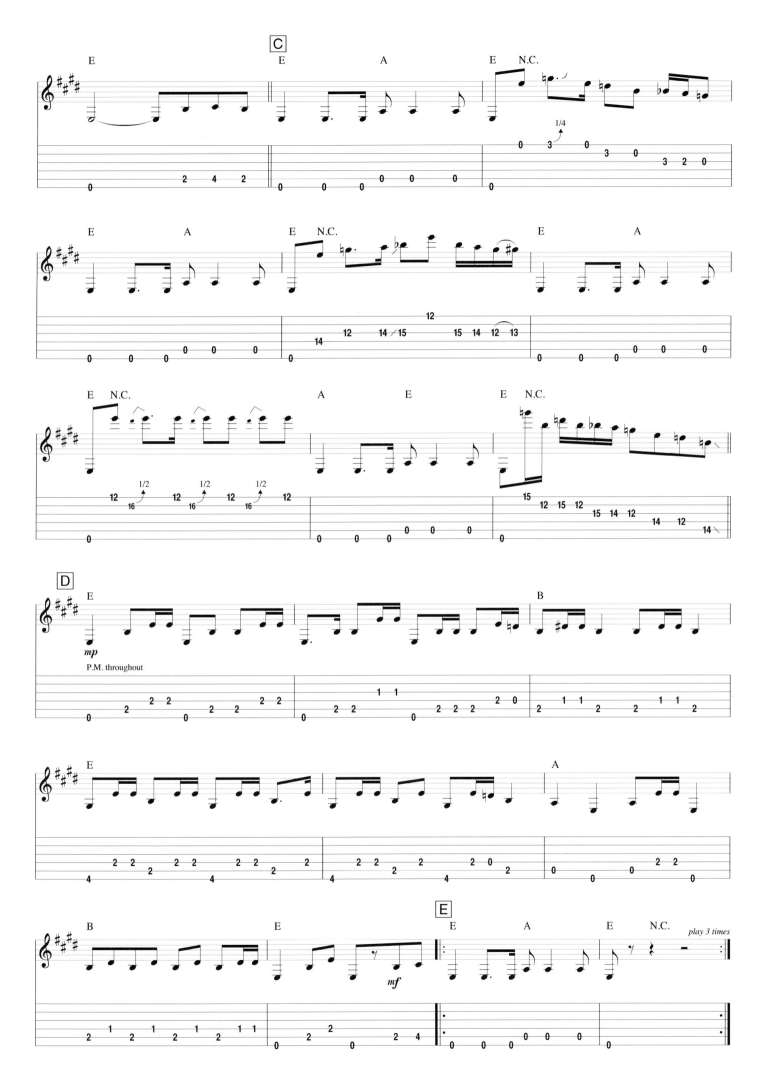

Yep!

By Duane Eddy and Lee Hazlewood

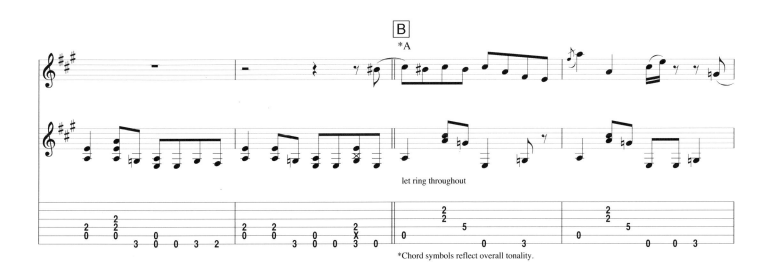

*Chord symbols reflect overall tonality.

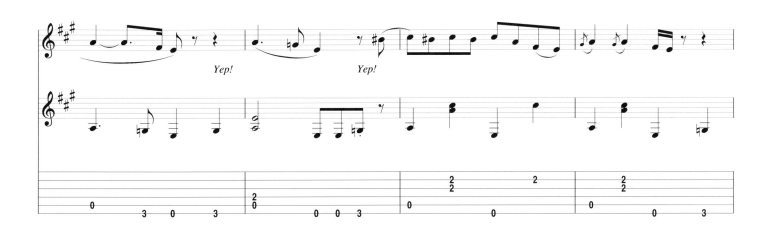

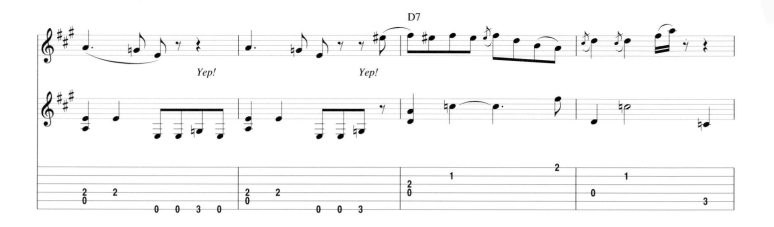

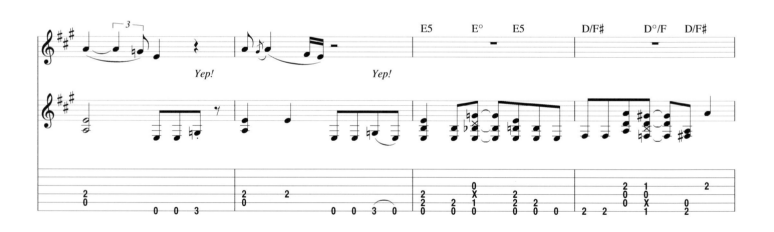

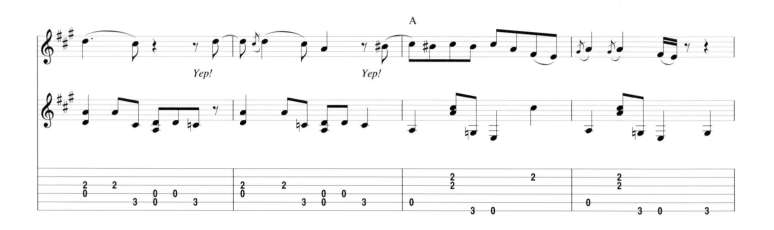

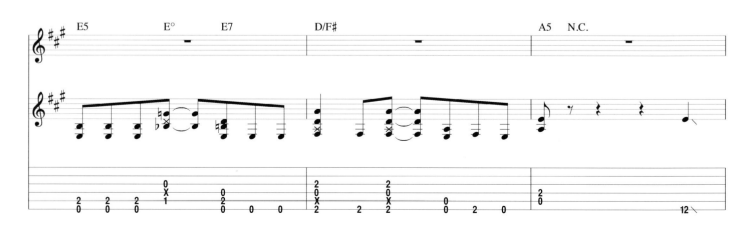

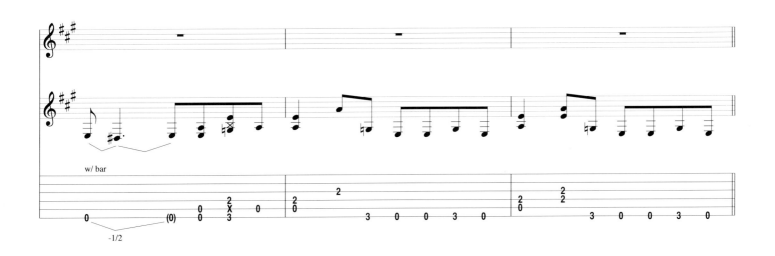

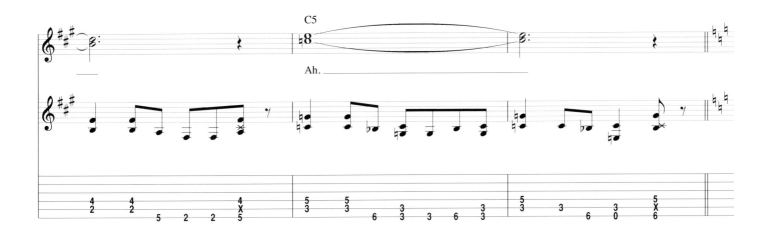

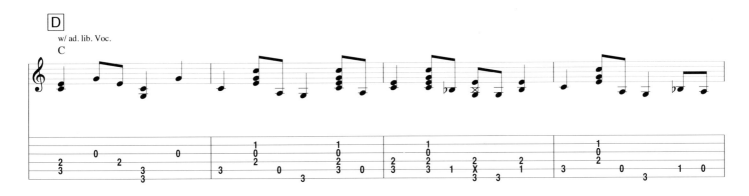

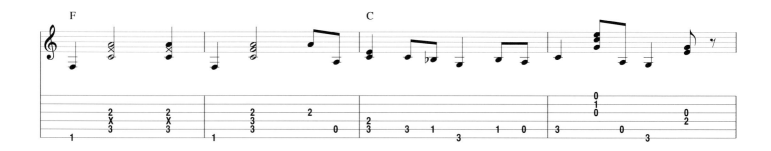

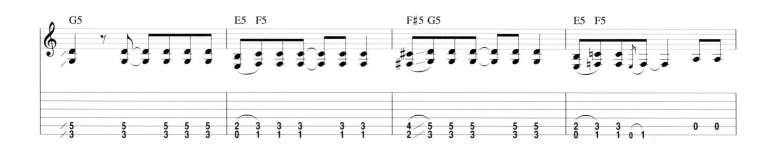

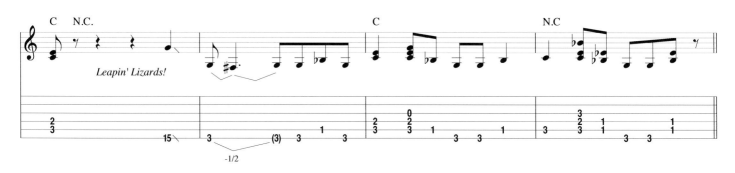

Leapin' Lizards!

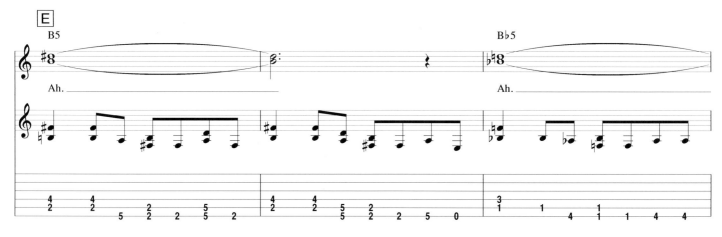

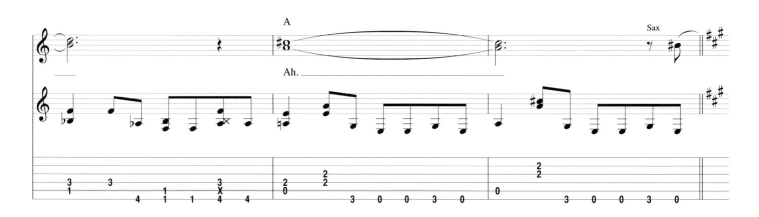

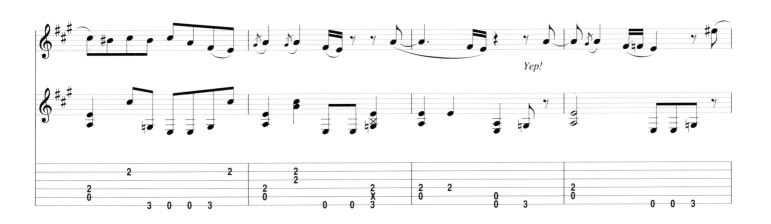

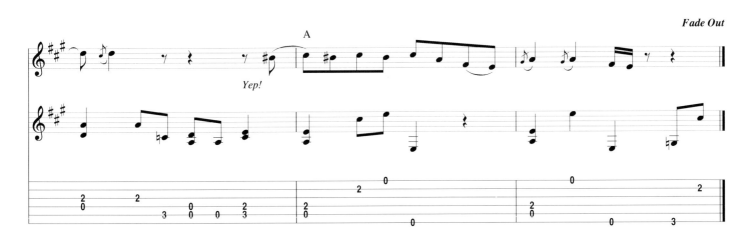

Three 30 Blues

By Duane Eddy and Lee Hazlewood

*Chord symbols reflect overall tonality.

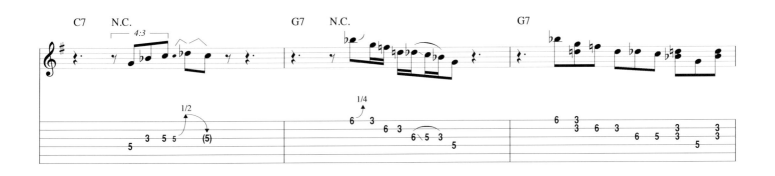

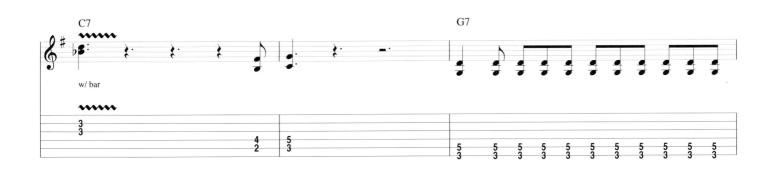

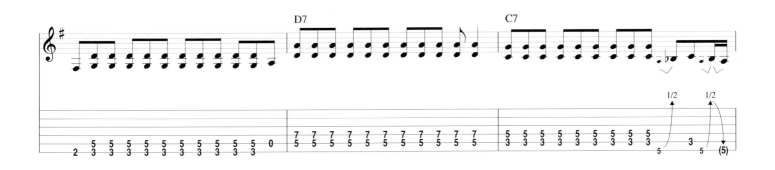

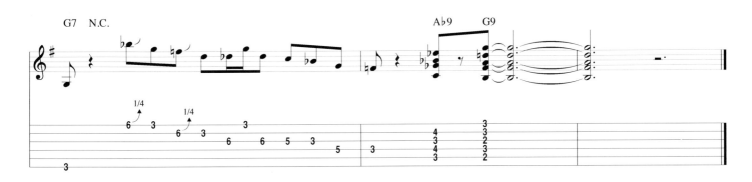

Trambone

By Chet Atkins

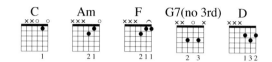